(Marc chAgАll

WHAT COLOUR IS PARADISE?

PRESTEL

Marc had one brother and several sisters, a father who was often sad and a mother who liked to laugh. Day in, day out, Mr. Chagall hauled heavy barrels around the fishmonger's where he worked while Mrs. Chagall used to sell turnips and flour in her little village shop. In the evening, when the two of them sat down together and the water for their tea was gurgling in the samovar, the parlour would be filled with the smell of herring salad.

Marc loved to clamber onto the roof and listen to the raucous cry of the ravens. He had narrow shoulders and unruly hair and was good at singing, dancing and playing the violin. By the age of ten he had already been learning Hebrew for several years at his religion classes. 'Lachlom,' he knew, means to dream.

In those days the little town of Vitebsk had thirty churches and more than sixty synagogues. Running past the paling fences and the brightly-painted wooden cottages, skirting the little gardens and the hens and the goats – this was the way Marc would take to the synagogue on feast days to listen to what the Prayer Leader had to say.

The Prayer Leader said:

"God created Man, in the likeness of God made He him; male and female created He them…"

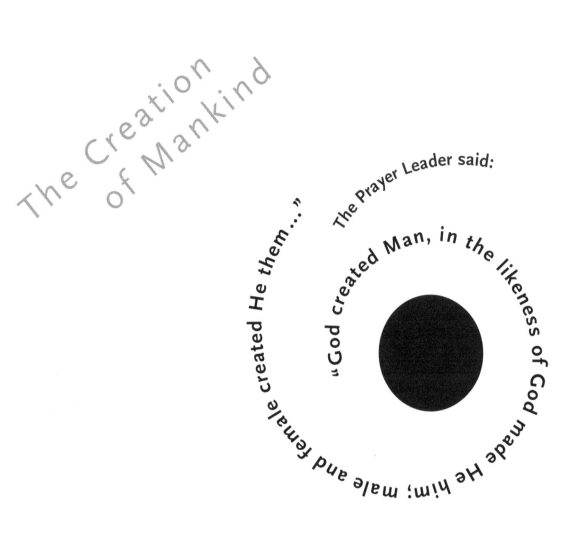

The red-coloured Wheel of Creation is spinning around, sending out c o l o u r s in all directions.

Marc later imagined the Wheel sending a huge rainbow out over Vitebsk and the Prayer Leader, over his father and mother. He imagined a creature – half human, half goat – sitting on the roof of the little village shop and a big fish swimming in a sea of sparkling gold. The Wheel splashes the slender figure on the cross with yellow and sprinkles the cockerel's feathers with red – which then comes to life and starts to dance around.

Gleaming with happiness an angel carries the first human being into the world

Once God had created the light and darkness, the sky and water, the oceans, the land and the flowers, the night and the day, the fish and the birds, He created the animals and mankind on the sixth day and, on the seventh, He rested. The seventh day was the Sabbath.

When Marc came back from the synagogue, the candles on the table would already have been lit for the Sabbath and the curtains drawn across the windows. "Holy Sabbath," said Marc and, in return, his parents would give him their blessing too. The clock on the wall ticked away; the candles burnt down slowly.

The Sabbath was the day of rest

When he was ten Marc wanted to be a violinist or a dancer but, instead, he was later to become a famous painter. He imagined two angels guiding the sun while below, floating in Paradise, he would see two goats, fish and human figures. This was the Creation.

What

colour

is

Paradise?

Painters

want

to

know.

Paradise

Paradise is a beautiful garden

Lines and bands of colour run across the lush green, still damp from the last rain. Under a half-moon and a greeny-golden sun life abounds. Birds are sitting in the trees, fish are swimming by and two sheep lower their soft, woolly heads to munch the grass. A blue goat, a purple bull and a green lion are all smiling contentedly. A big bird with shaggy feathers sails happily over a white cloud.

slowly upwards slides its way

Adam, bathed in golden yellow, shines out from among the green background and marvels at the miracle of the Creation. But Adam is lonely. An angel hurries to him, blowing gleefully on a trumpet. Adam shall not be lonely any longer.

Eve, tucked behind a cloud, is waiting for her companion. The couple hold each other tightly and are surrounded by a heart-shaped mass of flowers and fruit – a dazzling composition of colours. And God, the creator of all this splendour, brushes the heart of flowers in a gleaming flourish as he hovers over Adam and Eve.

The smiling snake

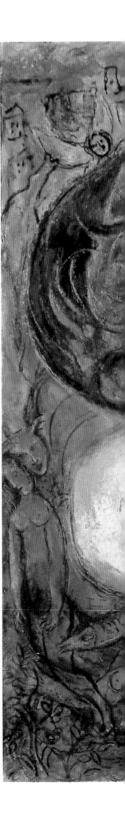

8

Eve looks at
the apple
in her hand.

How long will fortune last?

In Paradise humans and animals are very close to each other:

Adam and the spotted giraffe with its red nose – Eve and the red and blue-spangled peacock with its feathered train.

Life is heavenly.

Everything and everyone is in love and is dancing under the sun which is edged in green.

Bouquets of flowers are sailing through the blue sky.

Marc Chagall

"And the LORD GOD
planted a garden
eastward in Eden;
and there He put
the man whom
he had formed."

Bella was reading from the scriptures. She was Marc's wife and just a few years earlier Bella and Marc had married in Vitebsk. Their little daughter was called Ida. They were happy together and Marc painted a picture of himself and Bella bathed in a glowing light – a gleaming, golden colour like the sky over the town where they lived.

They often made long journeys together as a family, like the one to the Palestine – the Holy Land – where Marc could see the places described in the scriptures for himself.

"How
long
will
fortune
last?"

Bella asked herself.

"Everything darkened in front of my eyes,"

said Marc. As Bella lay dying in his arms, a violent thunderstorm with torrential rain passed over the house near New York where they were living. Marc was now alone in America with his daughter. Grief-stricken, he turned the pictures in his studio to face the wall.

It was wartime. Vitebsk and its synagogues lay in ruins and Marc's people were being murdered in gas chambers or were wandering from one country to another. For almost one whole year Marc did not paint any pictures.

Ida read aloud to her father:

"And they heard the voice

of the LORD GOD

walking in the garden

in the cool of the day."

The Expulsion from Paradise

In the middle of the Garden of Paradise stands the Tree of Knowledge on which the most beautiful apples grow. The tree is magnificent but Adam and Eve are not allowed to eat the fruit even though they would love to. Birds are fluttering around the tree and a yellow animal with crooked antlers is leaping through the undergrowth without a care in the world. Eve is not to blame – it is the snake that is so sly. It slithers up the trunk of the tree and whispers in Eve's ear to tempt her to take the apple. Paradise on earth is about to come to an end: first of all Eve eats the fruit of the Tree of Knowledge followed by Adam – who even feels much the worse for it. Their eyes become clear and Adam and Eve recognise the difference between good and evil which, until that time, only God had known. Now they both notice that they are naked and try to hide themselves from God.

"Where are you?"

God calls out to Adam.

Adam answers:

"I heard Thy voice in the garden, and I was afraid, because I was naked; and I hid myself.

God first curses the snake and then Adam and Eve and, since He does not want them to eat of the fruit on the Tree of Life as well, He expels them from Paradise.

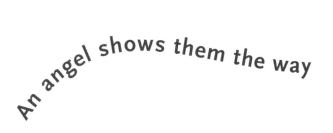

An angel shows them the way

Paradise has now been lost;

from now on life will be a burden. The beautiful Tree of Life glows like a golden bouquet of flowers. Fish and birds are circling around. One even has little horns which, as far as birds go, is most unusual. The air in the Garden of Paradise is filled with the scent of fresh green leaves, of flowers and sweet fruit.

For Man, however, Paradise has been lost and now dissolves into tears.

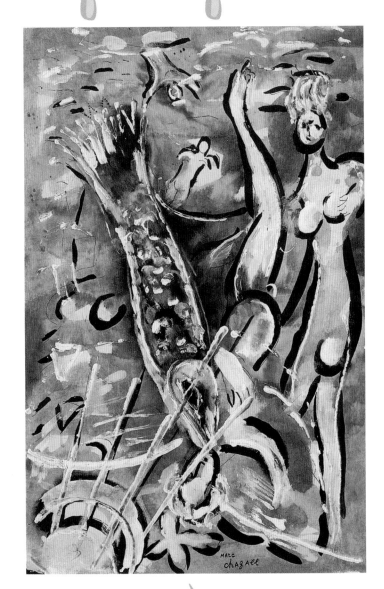

The flood washed away
all the colours in the world
and the earth grew pale.

Only grey and black and white were left behind.

But bobbing on the water's surface there was a ship made of wood. It was the ark, built by Noah who was a righteous man so that he and his family could be saved from the great flood.

God had ordered Noah to take two of every kind of animal onto his ark as well. As the waters rose over the blemished earth, Noah, his family and the animals were all safe and sound in the ark.

It rained and rained.

The waters rose and rose until they covered the highest mountain and touched the edge of the sky. All living creatures, both humans and animals, who were not on the ark, perished in the flood.

It rained and rained.

It rained and rained.

After many days and nights a wind passed over the earth and put an end to the furious flood. The ark came to rest at the top of the mountains of Ararat.

Noah opened a window and sent out a dove to see how far the waters had gone down.

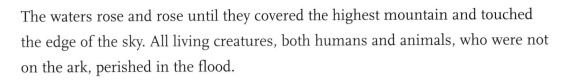

Noah's Ark

The inside of the ark is a safe haven for all forms of life, and all the colours of the rainbow have been saved too. Even the peacock with its spattering of reds and blues, has found a safe place in the ark. Noah gently strokes the goat's head, and a dove takes flight from his outstreched hand. The bright sky shines through the window into the depths of the ark.

Reds, yellows, and blues gleam in the greens of the very first Paradise.

People are holding each another tenderly, and the animals are all cuddled up closely.

All the animals and the humans are waiting patiently for the end of the flood.

Trustingly, the goat rubs up against Noah.

"And the dove came in to him in the evening; and lo, in her mouth was an olive leaf plucked off: so Noah knew that the waters were abated from off the earth. And he stayed yet other seven days; and sent forth the dove; which returned not again to him any more."
Vava, Marc's second wife, was reading to him.

The earth was now dry again.

Vava closed the book and looked out of the window. Marc and Vava were now living in the south of France. The weather was almost always good.

Vava brought back the joy into Marc's life which he had lost after Bella's death. Marc took Vava by the hand. A blue horse was galloping across the sky; someone was flying towards the sun and a bouquet of flowers was floating above the town.

Marc and Vava hugged each other

Life

One day Marc Chagall took a brush and paint and, once again, set the large, sun-shaped Wheel of Creation in motion on his canvas. He was almost eighty years old.

Street musicians

were playing their violins,

drums and trumpets.

It was a wonderful concert.

On the far left of the canvas he painted the parlour in his parents' home in Vitebsk with the blue bird from Paradise with its shaggy plumage circling overhead. For Marc, God was to be found in all people and things and so he mixed the stories in the scriptures with the everyday world which we can see around us – just like he mixed the colours on his palette. Three acrobats are performing handstands while another circus artist is balancing carefully on a tightrope. Moses is holding the tablets with the Commandments he received from God and, behind the huge fish, the ladder in Jacob's dream stretches up to heaven.

Again and again the Wheel of Creation sprays reds, yellows or greens onto the figures nearby. Bella, standing next to Marc with Ida in her arms, is pictured in her white wedding-dress. Marc painted a horse and cart and people fleeing from war and destruction. Next to the Eiffel Tower, the Tree of Life in the Garden of Paradise is full of colour. Vava is leaping through the air, dancing, and there is also a clown playing the cello.

There was laughter and tears, dancing and games, happiness, love and suffering. That's what life is.

Marc Chagall

was born on 7 July, 1887 in the Russian town of Vitebsk. His father worked at a fishmonger's and his mother ran a small shop. Marc was the eldest of nine children. For six years he attended the chedar – the Jewish primary school – before moving on to the local school. While he was there, he decided to become a painter. When he was seventeen he went to St. Petersburg and studied under the famous painter and stage-designer Léon Bakst. From 1910 to 1914 Marc lived in Paris and, shortly before the outbreak of World War I, the first major exhibition of his works was staged in Berlin. In the summer of 1915 he married Bella Rosenfeld whom he had already known for several years. In 1916 their daughter, Ida, was born. At first the family lived in Vitebsk where Marc founded an art school, before moving to Moscow, Berlin and Paris where they lived from 1923 onwards. In the meantime, Marc's fame was growing steadily. During the next few years he travelled frequently with his family. In 1931 they visited the Palestine where Marc could see the Holy Land for himself. Having been granted French citizenship in 1937, he then emigrated to America in 1941 where he was safe from the persecution of the Jews in Nazi Germany. During World War II Vitebsk was virtually completely destroyed. In the autumn of 1944 Bella died from a viral infection. Grief-stricken, Marc was not able to paint for many months. In 1948 he finally returned to Europe where he set up home in the south of France two years later. He continued to live there after his marriage to Valentina (Vava) Brodsky in 1952 until his death on 28 March, 1985. Marc Chagall was almost 98 years old.

In addition to his many paintings, he also created stained-glass windows, designed stage sets and illustrated books. One of the many things he loved was when someone read the scriptures out aloud. Many of Marc Chagall's paintings of religious scenes are now housed in a specially constructed musuem in Nice, in the south of France.